#DEARYOUNGPREACHER

A 31-DAY DEVOTIONAL FOR THE CALLED, THE COURAGEOUS, AND THE BECOMING

COREY A. MARCHAND SR.

Copyright © [2025] COREY A. MARCHAND SR.

All rights reserved. No part of this publication may be reproduced, stored in a retrieval system, or transmitted in any form or by any means—electronic, mechanical, photocopying, recording, or otherwise—without the prior written permission of the publisher, except in the case of brief quotations embodied in critical articles or reviews.

This book is a work of original authorship. While every effort has been made to ensure accuracy, the publisher and author assume no responsibility for errors or omissions or for the results obtained from the use of this material.

Published by Legacy Design

Cape Town, South Africa

publish@legacydesign.co.za

www.legacydesign

For permissions or bulk orders,

please contact publish@legacydesign.co.za or

whatsapp +27765068200

ISBN: 978-1-0492-0986-9

Printed in South Africa
First Edition

DEDICATION

To every young preacher who dared to say "yes" to God even when your voice trembled, your hands shook, and your heart questioned if you were enough—this is for you.

To the preacher who studies in secret, prays in silence, and serves in spaces where no one sees—your faithfulness is not forgotten.
To those who feel overlooked, underdeveloped,or misunderstood— keep going. God sees. God knows. God called you.

And finally, to the next generation of proclaimers, prophets, and pastors— may this devotional be your reminder that you were never called to perform, but to proclaim the good news with passion, purity, and power.

This is for every "yes" that cost you everything and every "still I rise" moment that followed. Stay faithful. Stay yielded. Stay anointed. The world needs your voice—but heaven needs your obedience.

#DearYoungPreacher, you were born for this!

FOREWORD

There is a weight in the whisper, a fire in the "yes," and a cross behind the call. Before robes ever flow and pulpits ever rise, there is a divine excavation, a private crucible where God forges the soul of the preacher through isolation, transformation, and obedience. This is not performance or charisma. This is consecration.

There comes a moment in every preacher's journey when the excitement of calling collides with the weight of responsibility. The pulpit may appear glorious, but the process behind it is often grueling. Ministry is beautiful, but it can also be burdensome. For those at the genesis of their journey, it can feel overwhelming, discerning God's voice while navigating the noise of opinion and the molding of one's soul. That's why #DearYoungPreacher is not just timely, it's necessary.

The story is told of a young preacher, fiery and full of zeal. He was invited to preach at a large conference, his first major platform. With a fresh suit and a pocket full of one-liners, he mounted the stage with swagger. His sermon stirred the crowd, but it lacked depth. It was more noise than nurture. Afterward, an elderly pastor pulled him aside and said, "You handled the mic well, son. But next time, try letting the Word handle you." It was a gentle rebuke, but it pierced like truth. That night, the young preacher wept, not from shame, but from awakening. He realized that the anointing is not just in how high you can shout, but how low you're willing to bow.

Humility is the hinge upon which anointing swings. Jesus made this clear in John 13, when He—Creator, Rabbi, and Messiah—wrapped Himself in a towel, knelt down, and washed the disciples' feet. Before the Last Supper, before the Garden, before the Cross, He served. "I have given you an example... do as I have done to you" (John 13:15). He taught that greatness in the Kingdom is not in how high you stand, but in how low you're willing to stoop.

In a time when social media platforms are mistaken for pulpits and notoriety is confused with calling, #DearYoungPreacher is a clarion call back to consecration. It whispers in the preacher's soul: God is not looking for stars. He's looking for servants.
In #DearYoungPreacher, Overseer Corey A. Marchand, Sr. writes as a man who has bled in the trenches of ministry. He writes not from a place of detached commentary, but from the deep wells of experiential theology, of one who has been through the fire, felt the silence, endured the crushing and still stands to say, "You're not alone." His pen is dipped in both pain and power. His wisdom is not theoretical, it is blood-tested, Spirit-breathed, and biblically anchored. In every line, there is the fragrance of Gethsemane and the fire of Pentecost.

Each daily excerpt in this 31-day journey offers a steady compass for the soul: a Scripture to anchor you, a prayer to shape you, a reflection to challenge you, and a word of affirmation to strengthen you. It's like having a mentor walk with you each day, helping you guard your heart while still giving God your full surrender. Whether you are preaching to hundreds or preparing in silence, this book is a timely antidote to ministry burnout, identity crisis, and spiritual stagnation.

Though titled #DearYoungPreacher, this devotional transcends chronology. It is not confined to age, but open to assignment. In Scripture, the call of God is never limited by biology, but always rooted in divine timing and spiritual readiness. Jeremiah was young when God said, "Do not say, 'I am only a youth,' for to all to whom I send you, you shall go" (Jeremiah 1:7). Yet Moses was eighty when his true ministry began at the burning bush. This devotional is not just for those young in years, but for those young in their "yes."

This is for the newly appointed pastor wrestling with imposter syndrome.

For the seasoned leader walking into a new mantle.

For the bivocational minister balancing pulpits and payrolls.

For the one preparing their first sermon, and the one preaching their last revival.

The call is not static, it evolves, and so must we.

In a world teetering on cultural chaos, post-pandemic fatigue, and a generation hungry for authenticity, God is raising up preachers who are not just eloquent, but holy. Not just visible, but rooted. Not just loud, but anointed.

Take your time. Sit with the lessons. Let the prayers guide you. Let the Scriptures root you. Let the reflections shape you. Because at the end of the day, this is not just about preaching sermons. It's about becoming the vessel God can use for His glory and the good of His people.

Remember this, the microphone may elevate your sound, but only submission will release your oil and the platform may give you a moment, but the mantle gives you a mission.

Walk this path with reverence. And let #DearYoungPreacher be your guide.

With great expectation,

Glenton O. Samuels, Jr., Ph.D.
Award-Winning Educator, Author, Professor and Pastor

Table of Contents

About The Author

Introduction

How to Use This Devotional

Part One: The Call and The Character

1. The Call Still Matters
2. Speak Even If You Tremble
3. Private Devotion Fuels Public Ministry
4. Stay Humble or You'll Stumble
5. Preparation is Worship
6. Preach with Purpose and Integrity
7. The Call and The Character

Part Two: The Discipline and the Development

8. It's Okay to Not Know Everything
9. Protect the Oil
10. You Don't Have to Compete
11. Don't Mistake Influence for Intimacy
12. It's Not About You
13. Learn to Rest Without Quitting
14. Grow Through What You Go Through

Part Three: The Weight and the Work

15. Character Will Carry What Charisma Cannot

16. Stay Teachable

17. The Pulpit Is Not a Performance Stage

18. Your Voice Matters

19. Be careful Who Lays Hands On You

20. Be an Answered Prayer, Not Just a Gifted Speaker

21. Don't Preach What You Don't Practice

Part Four: The Mission and the Mindset

22. Grace for the Gaps

23. Guard Your Private Life

24. Learn the Value of Silence

25. The Anointing Comes with a Cost

26. Ministry Is a Marathon, Not a Sprint

27. Honor the Assignment Even When It's Hard

28. Protect Your Friendships in Ministry

Part Five: The Finish and the Focus

29. Don't Get Caught Up in Comparison

30. Preach With Eternity in Mind

31. You Were Born for This

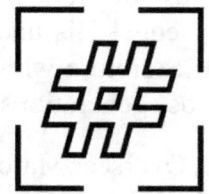

ABOUT THE AUTHOR

#DearYoungPreacher: A 31-Day Devotional

Overseer Corey A. Marchand Sr. is a dynamic voice and a devoted vessel in this generation, called to lead with conviction, teach with clarity, and preach with a prophetic edge. A native of Fort Lauderdale, Florida, he was lovingly "raised in the faith" by his late great-grandmother, Irene Roker, and mother, Sherlyn Marchand. As the oldest of four siblings—Alexis, Alyssa, and Anthony—Overseer Marchand's foundation was built on faith, reverence, and responsibility.

He accepted Jesus Christ at an early age and was baptized at New Hope Missionary Baptist Church under the leadership of Rev. Wilson Davis. His spiritual journey continued as he accepted his call to preach the Gospel of Jesus Christ and was licensed on November 25, 2001. On November 21, 2014, he was ordained as an Elder in the Lord's Church under the leadership of Bishop Albert Moore at Delray Community Missionary Baptist Church.

Today, Overseer Marchand serves as the proud Senior Pastor of The Center of Refuge in Port St. Lucie, Florida. He is a graduate of Trinity Theological Seminary and holds a Bachelor of Philosophy in Biblical Studies. With a ministry marked by passion, purpose, and prophetic insight, Overseer Marchand is often described as radical, revolutionary, innovative, anointed, and cutting edge. His uncommon ability to merge the timeless truths of Scripture with contemporary relevance empowers people across generations and cultures.

More than a preacher, Overseer Marchand is a visionary leader and a voice of wisdom and encouragement to young preachers across the nation. He is committed to cultivating the next wave of ministers and leaders, and #DearYoungPreacher is a testament to that commitment.

He is strengthened in life and ministry by his beautiful wife, Sister Deneisha Marchand, and together they are the proud parents of Corey Jr. and Cariah Marchand. Whether behind the pulpit, at a conference, or through the pages of this devotional, Overseer Marchand continues to inspire, challenge, and uplift those called to preach and lead in today's ever-changing world.

This devotional is not just a book—it's a call, a challenge, and a companion for the journey. To every young preacher: the pulpit is not your identity, but your assignment. Walk boldly, live righteously, and preach purposefully.

INTRODUCTION

Preaching is not just what we do—it's who we become in the hands of a Holy God.

#DearYoungPreacher, you are walking in a sacred calling that reaches beyond pulpits, platforms, and praise breaks. This calling is both weighty and wonderful, thrilling and terrifying. It demands more than just a good sermon—it demands a consecrated life.

I wrote this devotional for you!

For the preacher who's wrestling with insecurity but still says "yes."

For the one who's full of fire but still learning how to carry it.

For the one who wonders, "Am I called enough? Anointed enough? Ready enough?"

This is not just encouragement—it's fuel. Each day is crafted to stir your spirit, sharpen your focus, and strengthen your walk. You'll be challenged to grow in character, deepen your devotion, and preach with clarity, conviction, and compassion.

The goal isn't to become famous.

The goal is to become faithful.

In this devotional, you won't find formulas—you'll find fire. Not hype, but hope. You'll discover that your call is not based on your perfection but on God's purpose. You'll be reminded that private obedience always precedes public power.

So lean in!

Let these 31 days mark a shift in your mindset, your ministry, and your maturity.

Let God build the preacher—not just the platform.

This journey is for the young in age, the young at heart, and the young in ministry. If you've got a "yes" in your spirit and a call on your life, then this devotional is for you.

Let's grow together.

How to Use This Devotional

Welcome to #DearYoungPreacher. Whether you're standing at the starting line of your calling or you've already been preaching for some time, this 31-day journey is designed to help you grow deeper in character, stronger in conviction, and bolder in purpose.

This devotional is not just something to read—it's something to experience. Each day has been prayerfully written to speak directly to your heart, challenge your discipline, and stir up the gift within you. Here's how to make the most of your time with it:

1. Start With Expectation

Approach each day with an open heart. Expect God to speak. He desires to meet with you—not just through the pulpit, but through quiet, personal moments of devotion.

2. Read Slowly and Prayerfully

Each daily entry includes a focused Scripture, a devotional thought, encouragement, a prayer, and a meditation prompt. Don't rush through it. Take your time. Reflect deeply. Let the words speak to where you are right now.

3. Respond Authentically

After each devotional, there's space to respond. Journal your honest thoughts. Write prayers, confessions, sermon ideas, or anything the Holy Spirit lays on your heart. This is your sacred space to process and grow.

4. Build a Rhythm

Choose a consistent time and place to meet with God every day. Whether it's early in the morning, during a lunch break, or late at night, consistency creates momentum. Try to complete one entry per day for 31 days, but give yourself grace. If you need to pause and sit with one entry longer, do it.

5. Revisit and Reflect

This book isn't just for one-time use. Come back to it. Mark it up. Highlight what stands out. Months or years from now, you'll look back and see how far God has brought you. You are not just a preacher—you are a vessel.

God is forming, filling, and using you. This devotional is just one tool He's using to strengthen your voice and sharpen your vision. So lean in. Listen closely. The world needs your voice, but more than that—it needs your obedience.

Let the journey begin!

#DAY 1: THE CALL STILL MATTERS

"Before I formed you in the womb I knew you, before you were born I set you apart; I appointed you as a prophet to the nations." —Jeremiah 1:5 (NIV)

Devotional Thought:

#DearYoungPreacher, your call is not a coincidence—it is divine and deliberate. Before you ever preached your first sermon or recognized your own voice, God had already ordained your steps. There will be moments when you question your qualifications or feel overlooked. But your call was never based on human approval—it was God's idea before time began.

Don't downplay the call just because it's not celebrated yet. God doesn't call the qualified—He qualifies the called. The call still matters when your calendar is empty. It still matters when your name isn't on a flyer. It still matters when the enemy tells you you're not enough.

Encouragement:

The fact that you're called means you're needed. You are God's answer to someone's spiritual drought. God didn't just call you—He chose you.

Prayer:

Father, thank You for choosing me. Remind me daily that I am not an accident or an afterthought. Help me to walk in confidence, not arrogance, knowing that You have appointed me for a purpose. Strengthen me when I feel small and encourage me when I feel unseen. In Jesus' name, amen.

Meditation Prompt:

Take 10 minutes today to sit with this truth: "I am called, I am chosen, I am seen." Breathe deeply and let it settle in your spirit.

Respond:

Write down the moment you first felt or heard your call to preach. What were the circumstances? How did you feel? Where were you spiritually? Revisit that moment and thank God for it.

_____

_____

_____

_____

_____

_____

_____

DAY 2: SPEAK EVEN IF YOU TREMBLE

"Now go; I will help you speak and will teach you what to say." —Exodus 4:12 (NIV)

Devotional Thought:

#DearYoungPreacher, fear doesn't disqualify you—silence does. Moses tried to discredit himself because of a stutter, but God didn't remove his weakness—He gave him grace to speak through it. Your hesitation doesn't cancel your calling. If God called you, He'll help you.

It's okay to tremble. It's okay to feel nervous. Just don't let fear keep you from speaking truth. Your obedience is more powerful than your insecurity. Every time you stand to speak, Heaven stands behind you.

Encouragement:

You don't have to be eloquent—you just have to be obedient. Speak up. The message is greater than your fears.

Prayer:

Lord, I admit I feel nervous sometimes. I want to honor You with my words, but I also want to get it right. Remind me that it's not about perfection, it's about obedience. Help me trust Your voice above my fears. In Jesus' name, amen.

Meditation Prompt:

What fear do you need to surrender today in order to obey God fully?

Respond:

Write a short prayer of courage. Keep it close. Read it before you preach or teach.

_____

_____

_____

_____

_____

_____

_____

_____

_____

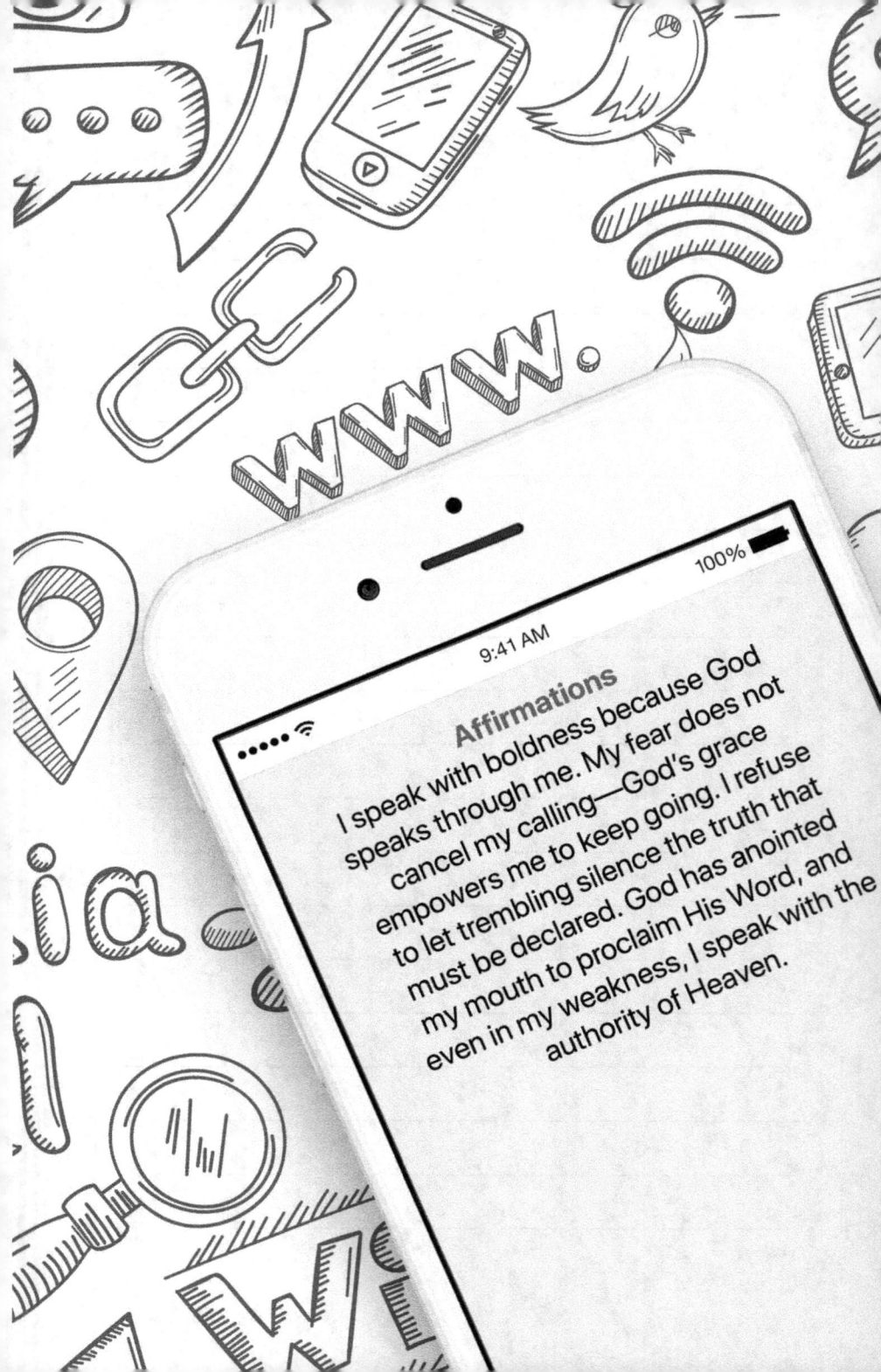

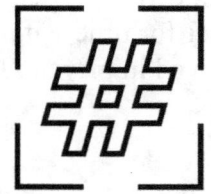

DAY 3: PRIVATE DEVOTION FUELS PUBLIC MINISTRY

"But Jesus often withdrew to lonely places and prayed." — Luke 5:16 (NIV)

Devotional Thought:

#DearYoungPreacher, what you do in private shapes what you carry in public. The secret place is where sermons are born, burdens are lifted, and power is replenished. Don't get so busy preparing to preach that you forget to pray.

The oil flows where intimacy dwells. Preaching without prayer is like shouting through a mic with no power—it's just noise. When you've been with God, people can tell.

Encouragement:

Preaching without private devotion is dangerous. Build the habit of hiding away with God. He speaks the loudest in stillness.

Prayer:

Lord, teach me to value Your presence more than the platform. Create in me a hunger for time with You. Don't let me preach what I haven't first lived in private. In Jesus' name, amen.

Meditation Prompt:

Where in your schedule can you consistently meet with God with no distractions?

Respond:

Create a weekly plan for consistent private devotion—even 15–20 minutes daily.

_____

_____

_____

_____

_____

_____

_____

_____

_____

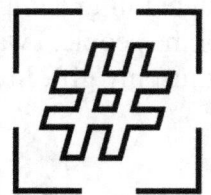

DAY 4: STAY HUMBLE OR YOU'LL STUMBLE

"God opposes the proud but shows favor to the humble." — James 4:6 (NIV)

Devotional Thought:

#DearYoungPreacher, never get so good at preaching that you forget the God who called you. Pride is sneaky. It shows up when the crowd claps, when your name is recognized, or when you think you don't need help anymore.

Humility isn't weakness—it's wisdom. God resists the proud. You don't want to be resisted by the same God who called you. Stay low. Serve well. Remember: the higher you go, the deeper your roots must grow.

Encouragement:

You are not the main character—Jesus is. Stay usable by staying humble.

Prayer:

Lord, keep me grounded in grace. Let me never exalt myself above the message or the people. I want to be known in Heaven for my humility, not just my gift. In Jesus' name, amen.

Meditation Prompt:

When was the last time you invited feedback or correction?

Respond:

Write down three ways you can guard your heart from pride this week.

_____

_____

_____

_____

_____

_____

_____

_____

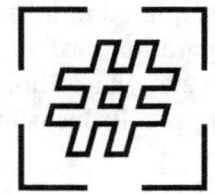

DAY 5: PREPARATION IS WORSHIP

"Do your best to present yourself to God as one approved, a worker who does not need to be ashamed and who correctly handles the word of truth." —2 Timothy 2:15 (NIV)

Devotional Thought:

#DearYoungPreacher, study is not just academic—it's spiritual. Your preparation is an act of worship. When you labor in the Word, when you search the Scriptures, when you seek the Spirit's guidance for the message—it pleases God.

Don't study just to impress—study to impart. It's not about sounding deep; it's about being deeply rooted. God honors your time in preparation. Even when no one sees the hours you put in, Heaven does.

Encouragement:

What you feed on in private becomes the bread you serve to others. Study with hunger. Preach from overflow.

Prayer:

Father, give me a disciplined mind and a hungry heart. Let me never approach preparation casually. May my time in study lead me to deeper revelation and holy conviction. Teach me to handle Your Word rightly. In Jesus' name, amen.

Meditation Prompt:

What does your current preparation routine look like? How can you grow it?

Respond:

Write down a study goal for this week. Maybe it's one chapter, one word study, or one new book.

_____

_____

_____

_____

_____

_____

_____

_____

_____

Affirmations

My preparation honors God and equips me to serve with excellence. I study with diligence so I can preach with clarity, knowing that the Holy Spirit reveals truth as I create space through disciplined study. I am becoming a faithful student of the Word, committed to growing in understanding and wisdom. Every hour I invest in study is not wasted—is an act of both obedience and worship unto God.

Day 6: PREACH WITH PURPOSE AND INTEGRITY

"Woe to you when everyone speaks well of you, for that is how their ancestors treated the false prophets." —Luke 6:26 (NIV)

"Watch your life and doctrine closely. Persevere in them, because if you do, you will save both yourself and your hearers." —1 Timothy 4:16 (NIV)

Devotional Thought:

#DearYoungPreacher, the pulpit is not a platform for popularity—it is a place of sacred proclamation. We are not called to be performers who seek applause, but prophetic voices who carry Heaven's message. When we trade conviction for compliments, we lose the very power that makes our preaching impactful.

But it's not just about what we say—it's about how we live. Your sermon begins long before you take the mic. Your lifestyle is your first message. Integrity is what gives weight to your words and substance to your sound. A preacher with gifting but no godliness is a danger, not a blessing.

People will hear your voice, but they will also examine your walk. Preach with power, yes—but live with purity. Let your life confirm your sermon, not contradict it. Your credibility is built in private before it's ever displayed in public.

Encouragement:
Be faithful, not flashy. Let the Word be the main attraction. God is more concerned with your holiness than your homiletics. Stay real. Stay grounded. Stay accountable.

Prayer:
Lord, check my heart before I step into the pulpit. Let me never treat the sacred as common. May my motives be pure and my message be Yours. Help me to live with integrity so that my life backs up my words. Guard me from secret compromise. In Jesus' name, amen.

Meditation Prompt:
What is your heart posture before you preach? Are you seeking to impact lives or impress people? Where do you need accountability to align your life with your message?

Respond:
Write a personal statement or prayer you will say before every sermon to center your motives and ground your integrity. Also, identify one spiritually mature person to help keep you accountable this month.

_____

_____

_____

Affirmations

I preach for transformation, not attention, and I strive to ensure that my life reflects the very truth I proclaim. The pulpit is a place of purpose, not performance, and I approach it with reverence and responsibility. I choose character over charisma, valuing integrity more than applause. I am trustworthy with the message because I am fully submitted to the Messenger—Jesus Christ.

DAY 7: THE CALL AND THE CHARACTER

"So he shepherded them according to the integrity of his heart, and guided them by the skillfulness of his hands." — Psalm 78:72 (NKJV)

Devotional Thought:

#DearYoungPreacher, the weight of your call isn't just in what you do—but in who you are. God doesn't just anoint the gift; He examines the vessel. We're called not only to preach powerfully, but to live purely. Culture celebrates charisma, but Heaven still seeks character.

David wasn't chosen just for his harp or sling, but for his heart. His leadership stood on integrity and skill. The call of God is holy—it requires our character to match our message, and our lifestyle to align with our confession.

Before you stand to preach, kneel in His presence. Talent may open doors, but only character sustains credibility.

The anointing is no excuse for arrogance, and the call is no cover for compromise. God desires a surrendered life, not just a strong voice. Who you are matters just as much as what you say.

Encouragement:

You don't have to be perfect, but you must be **surrendered**. God's grace is not a license to live loosely—it's power to live holy. Your private disciplines shape your public effectiveness. Integrity is not optional—it is essential. Let God refine you in secret so He can trust you in the spotlight.

Prayer:

Father, thank You for calling me to Your work. Help me to walk worthy of the calling. Purge my heart of pride, hypocrisy, and compromise. Build in me the kind of character that honors You. Let my life preach louder than my sermons. In Jesus' name, amen.

Meditation:

What are the areas in my life where my character needs to catch up to my calling? Where do I need to grow in integrity and discipline?

Response Prompt:

Today, write a private letter to God about the kind of preacher—and person—you desire to become. Be honest. Be specific. Then ask Him to help you become that individual, day by day.

_____

_____

_____

Affirmations

I am called by God and being continually shaped by His hand. I choose to let my character align with my calling, refusing to let compromise define me. Integrity matters more than image, and I welcome God's refining work in my life—for His glory, not mine. It is my private obedience that fuels and sustains my public ministry.

DAY 8: IT'S OKAY TO NOT KNOW EVERYTHING

"For we know in part and we prophesy in part." —1 Corinthians 13:9 (NIV)

Devotional Thought:

#DearYoungPreacher, you are not expected to know it all. Growth takes time. Revelation comes layer by layer. Don't let the pressure to have all the answers push you into performance or pride. There is strength in admitting, "I don't know, but I'm learning."

The greatest preachers are lifelong students. Never stop asking questions. Never stop learning. Let humility lead your hunger for truth.

Encouragement:

God doesn't need you to be perfect—He just needs you to be teachable.

Prayer:

Father, thank You for being patient with me. Help me to remain humble, hungry, and open to learning. Give me the grace to admit what I don't know, and the courage to keep growing. In Jesus' name, amen.

Meditation Prompt:

What's one area of Scripture or doctrine you feel unsure about? Ask God for wisdom today.

Respond:

Write down 2–3 topics you'd like to study more deeply over the next month.

_____

_____

_____

_____

_____

_____

_____

_____

_____

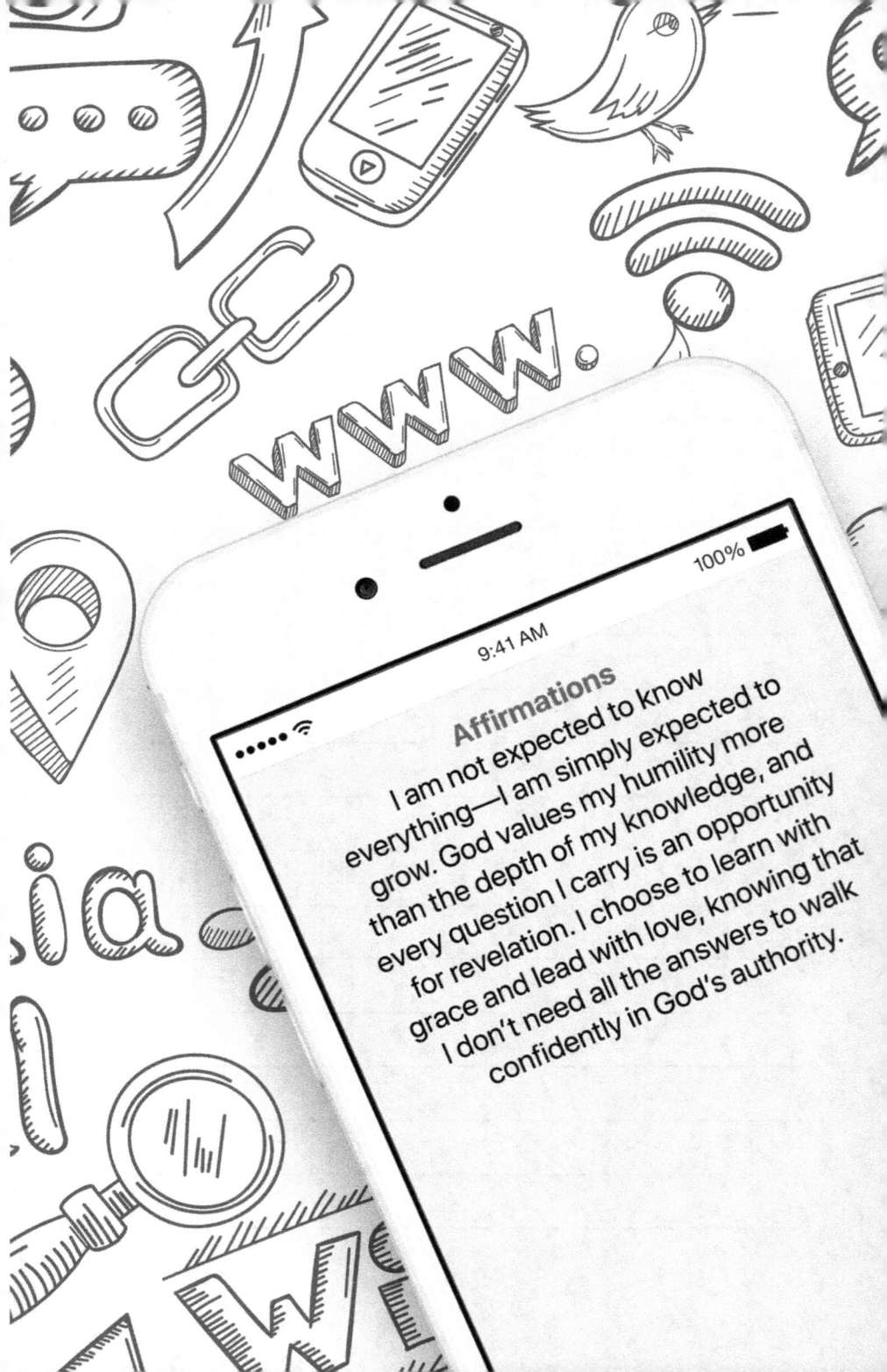

Affirmations

I am not expected to know everything—I am simply expected to grow. God values my humility more than the depth of my knowledge, and every question I carry is an opportunity for revelation. I choose to learn with grace and lead with love, knowing that I don't need all the answers to walk confidently in God's authority.

DAY 9: PROTECT THE OIL

"But the wise ones took oil in jars along with their lamps." — Matthew 25:4 (NIV)

Devotional Thought:

#DearYoungPreacher, the anointing is costly. It will cost you your pride, your plans, and your preferences. Don't waste it. Don't trade it. Don't cheapen it. The oil is for God's glory, not your platform.

Protect your oil by guarding your time, your heart, your eyes, and your ears. Protect it by saying "no" to what doesn't align with your purpose. Everyone won't understand your discipline—but your destiny depends on it.

Encouragement:

You are carrying something sacred. Treat it like treasure, not trash.

Prayer:

Lord, help me to steward the oil you have placed on my life. Don't let me take it lightly. Teach me to guard my heart and walk in wisdom. Keep me sensitive to Your Spirit. In Jesus' name, amen.

Meditation Prompt:

Ask yourself: What habits or relationships may be draining the oil God gave me?

Respond:

Identify one distraction you need to set boundaries around this week.

_____

_____

_____

_____

_____

_____

_____

_____

_____

_____

_____

Affirmations

I carry oil, and I will guard it with both discipline and discernment. My anointing is not for performance, but for divine purpose, and I refuse to waste what cost me everything to carry. God can trust me to protect what He has poured into me. I am a wise vessel—filled, prepared, and ready to be used for His glory.

DAY 10: YOU DON'T HAVE TO COMPETE

"A man can receive only what is given him from heaven." — John 3:27 (NIV)

Devotional Thought:

#DearYoungPreacher, comparison is a trap, and competition is a lie. There is room for you without you needing to replace someone else. Your calling has its own lane, its own pace, and its own impact.

Don't measure your progress by someone else's platform. God doesn't run out of purpose. The Kingdom is not a contest—it's a collaboration.

Encouragement:

Celebrate others without shrinking yourself. Stay focused. Stay faithful. Your lane has been custom-designed for you.

Prayer:

Father, help me to run my race with joy. Deliver me from jealousy, envy, or insecurity. Let me be confident in the portion You've assigned to me. Remind me that I don't have to compete—I'm already chosen. In Jesus' name, amen.

Meditation Prompt:

Whose success have you secretly envied? Surrender that to God and ask Him to bless them.

Respond:

Write a thank-you note or message to another young preacher who inspires you. Celebrate them intentionally.

_____

_____

_____

_____

_____

_____

_____

_____

_____

_____

_____

Affirmations

I have my own lane, and I am committed to running it well. In God's Kingdom, there is no competition—only collaboration and unity. I trust that God's timing for my life is perfect, so I don't rush or compare myself to others. I celebrate the success of others while staying confident and focused on my unique calling. I'm not competing—I'm called

DAY 11: DON'T MISTAKE INFLUENCE FOR INTIMACY

"Many will say to me on that day, 'Lord, Lord, did we not prophesy in your name...?' Then I will tell them plainly, 'I never knew you.'" —Matthew 7:22–23 (NIV)

Devotional Thought:

#DearYoungPreacher, just because people know your name doesn't mean Heaven knows your voice. It's possible to be influential and still disconnected from the One who called you. Your gift can open doors, but only intimacy with God keeps you anchored behind them.

Don't let ministry become a substitute for relationship. Don't get so busy preaching that you forget to pray. Your public platform is sustained by your private connection.

Encouragement:

The goal isn't to be seen—it's to stay close. Influence without intimacy is empty.

Prayer:

Lord, don't let me confuse doing things for You with being with You. I desire to walk closely with You, not just to serve from afar. Draw me near daily and let intimacy be my greatest pursuit. In Jesus' name, amen.

Meditation Prompt:

Is there anything in your routine that has replaced or reduced your time with God?

Respond:

Plan a quiet retreat—even if it's just a few hours—to spend uninterrupted time in prayer and worship.

_____

_____

_____

_____

_____

_____

_____

_____

_____

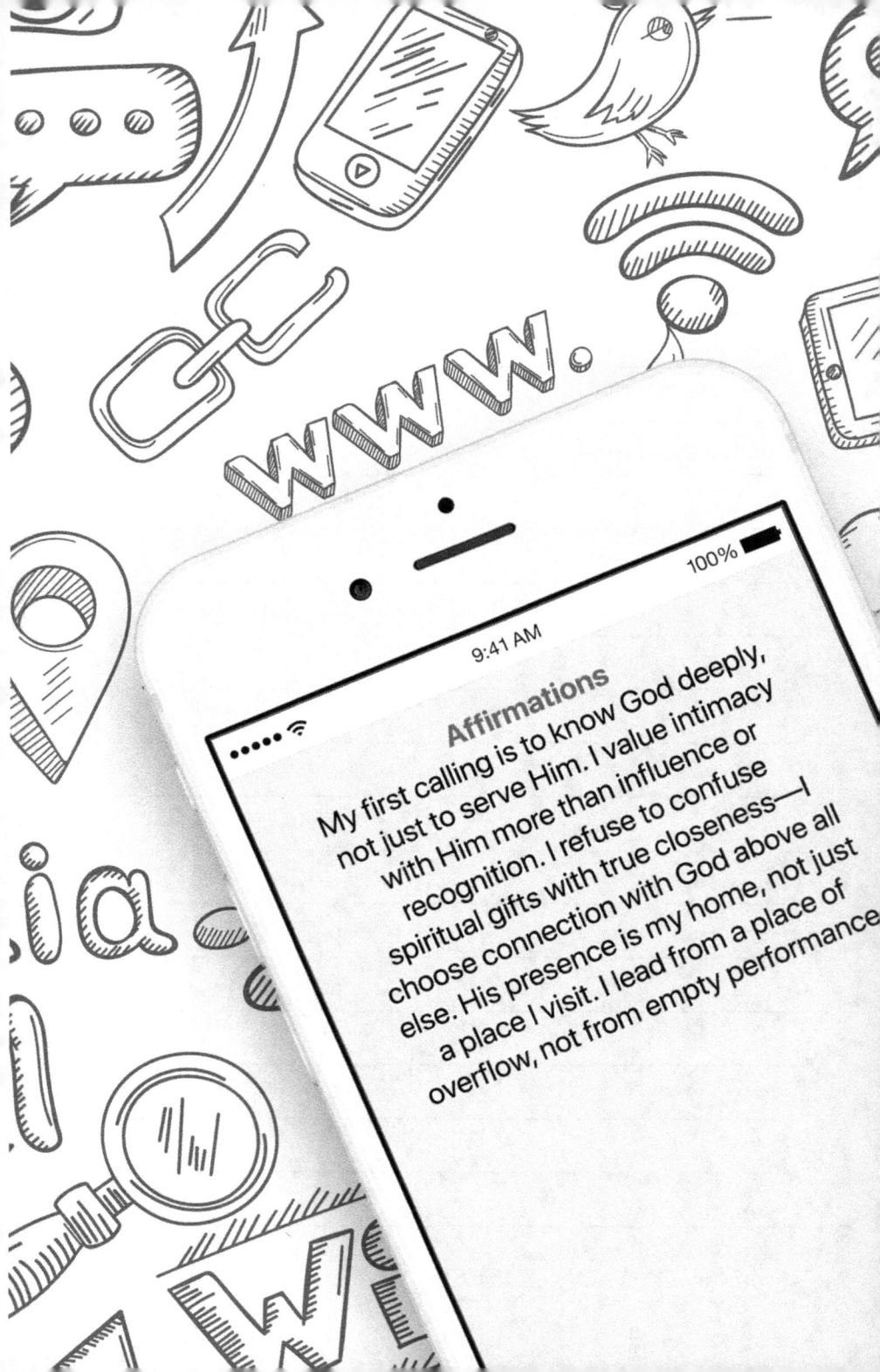

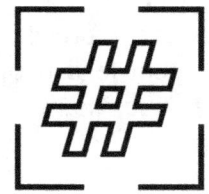

DAY 12: IT'S NOT ABOUT YOU

"He must become greater; I must become less." —John 3:30 (NIV)

Devotional Thought:

#DearYoungPreacher, the pulpit is not your pedestal. Ministry is not your spotlight. It's never been about your name, your brand, or your moment—it's about Jesus. He must increase. You must decrease.

God doesn't share glory. You are a vessel, not the source. When you point people to Jesus instead of to yourself, you become a trustworthy ambassador of the Kingdom.

Encouragement:

Stay small in your own eyes so that God can be seen clearly through your life.

Prayer:

Father, remove any pride, ego, or need to be seen from my heart. Let every message I preach, every post I share, and every assignment I accept lead people to Jesus—not me. Be glorified in all I do. In Jesus' name, amen.

Meditation Prompt:

Who gets the credit when your ministry succeeds—God or you?

Respond:

Audit your last three public ministry moments (sermons, posts, prayers). Were they Jesus-centered or self-promoting?

_____
_____
_____
_____
_____
_____
_____
_____
_____
_____
_____

Affirmations

I am a vessel, and Jesus is the message I carry. I decrease so that Christ may increase through me. My platform exists for His glory, not for personal gain or recognition. I stay low so that God can be lifted high, keeping Jesus at the center of my calling—not my ego.

DAY 13: LEARN TO REST WITHOUT QUITTING

"Come to me, all you who are weary and burdened, and I will give you rest." —Matthew 11:28 (NIV)

Devotional Thought:

#DearYoungPreacher, burnout is not a badge of honor. Ministry is demanding, but God never asked you to sacrifice your soul to serve Him. You need rest. You are not failing if you step back to recover.

Rest doesn't mean you're quitting. It means you're honoring your limits and trusting God to work even when you're not. Sabbath is not optional—it's sacred.

Encouragement:

You can't pour from an empty cup. Take care of your soul before you try to save others.

Prayer:

God, teach me how to rest without guilt. Help me to know when to work and when to be still. Heal the places in me that are tired, weary, and worn. Fill me again with strength and peace. In Jesus' name, amen.

Meditation Prompt:

What drains you the most in this season of ministry? When was your last real rest?

Respond:

Plan a Sabbath day or weekend this month. Unplug. Be still. Let God refill you.

_____

_____

_____

_____

_____

_____

_____

_____

_____

DAY 14: GROW THROUGH WHAT YOU GO THROUGH

"Consider it pure joy, my brothers and sisters, whenever you face trials of many kinds, because you know that the testing of your faith produces perseverance." —James 1:2–3 (NIV)

Devotional Thought:

#DearYoungPreacher, your trials are not random—they're refining. Every test has a lesson. Every hardship has a purpose. You may be walking through fire now, but know this: the fire is forming you.

Preachers are not made in the pulpit—they are made in the press. Don't just go through it. Grow through it. Let your tears teach. Let your trials mature you. Let your wilderness increase your wisdom.

Encouragement:

The trial you're in today is equipping you for the platform tomorrow. You're being strengthened for what's next.

Prayer:

Father, thank You for the strength to endure what I don't understand. Grow me in the fire. Teach me in the trial. Let nothing I go through be wasted. Use it all for my good and for Your glory. In Jesus' name, amen.

Meditation Prompt:

How is this current season challenging you? What might God be trying to teach you through it?

Respond:

Journal what this current challenge is producing in you—patience, trust, faith, humility?

_____

_____

_____

_____

_____

_____

_____

_____

_____

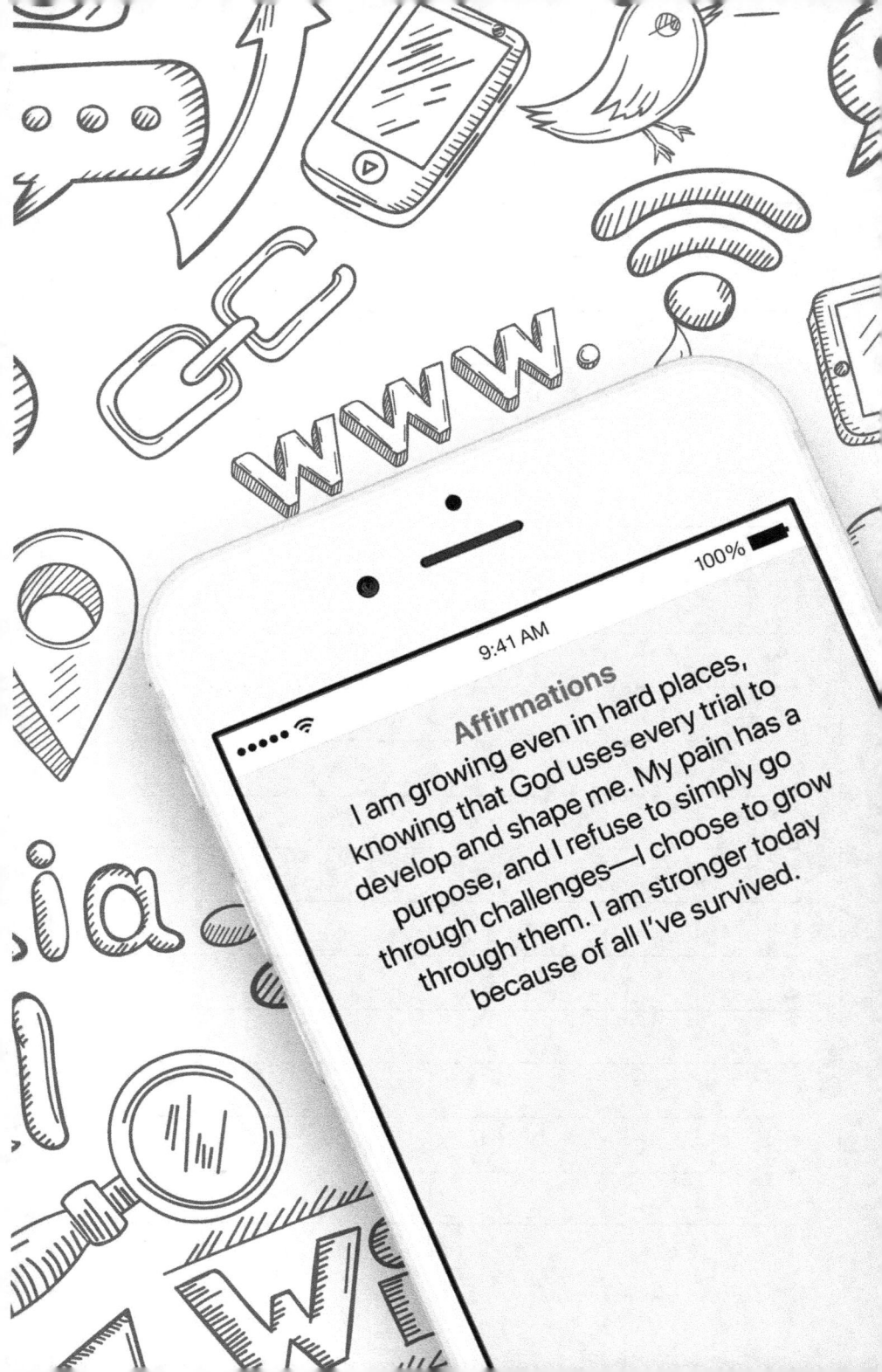

DAY 15: CHARACTER WILL CARRY WHAT CHARISMA CANNOT

"The integrity of the upright guides them, but the unfaithful are destroyed by their duplicity." —Proverbs 11:3 (NIV)

Devotional Thought:

#DearYoungPreacher, your gift may open doors, but only your character will keep them open. Don't let charisma take you places that your integrity can't sustain you. Who you are off the platform matters more than what you do on it.

You don't need to be perfect—but you do need to be pure. Choose honesty over hype. Choose humility over applause. Choose truth over performance. The oil flows where the character is clean.

Encouragement:

Let your private life be as powerful as your public presentation. Character is the currency of trust.

Prayer:

God, refine my heart and purify my motives. Make me whole in the dark so I can walk with integrity in the light. Help me build a life that is solid, not just seen. In Jesus' name, amen.

Meditation Prompt:

Where is your character being tested right now? What do you need to surrender?

Respond:

Choose one private habit you want to strengthen this week to grow your character. My private purity fuels my public power.

DAY 16: STAY TEACHABLE

"Let the wise listen and add to their learning, and let the discerning get guidance." —Proverbs 1:5 (NIV)

Devotional Thought:

#DearYoungPreacher, don't ever outgrow correction. You may be called, but you're still being formed. Stay teachable. Stay open. Stay submitted to wise voices that can speak into your blind spots.

Being teachable doesn't make you weak—it makes you wise. Surround yourself with people who love you enough to correct you. Don't just gather fans. Gather mentors, coaches, and truth-tellers.

Encouragement:

The greatest leaders are lifelong learners. There's always more to know and more to grow.

Prayer:

Father, give me a heart that receives instruction and correction. Remove pride and help me stay open to wisdom, even when it stings. Surround me with voices that sharpen me. In Jesus' name, amen.

Meditation Prompt:

When was the last time you received correction? How did you respond?

Respond:

Reach out to a mentor or elder and ask them one thing they see in you that you can grow in.

_____

_____

_____

_____

_____

_____

_____

_____

_____

_____

_____

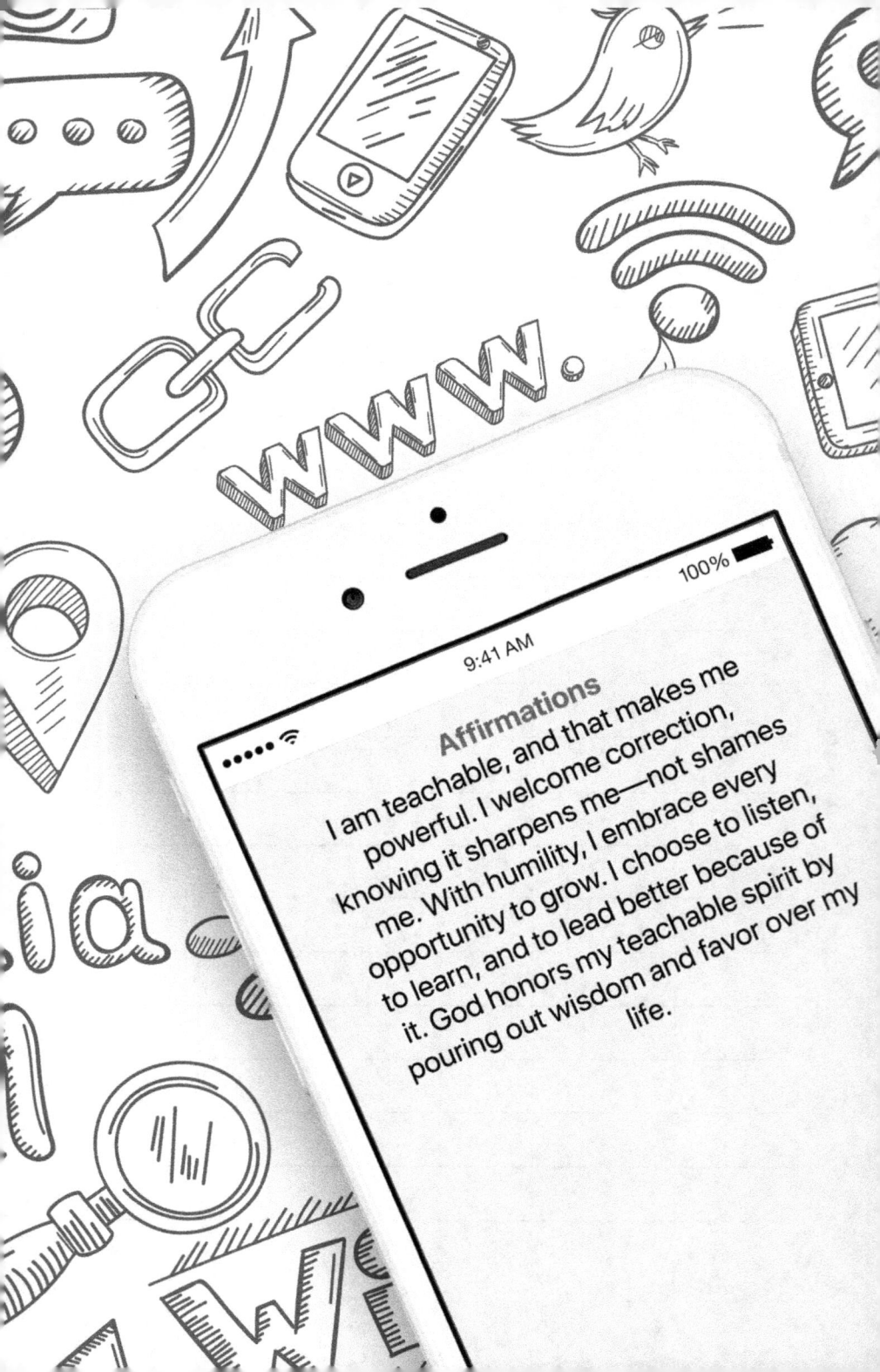

Affirmations

I am teachable, and that makes me powerful. I welcome correction, knowing it sharpens me—not shames me. With humility, I embrace every opportunity to grow. I choose to listen, to learn, and to lead better because of it. God honors my teachable spirit by pouring out wisdom and favor over my life.

DAY 17: THE PULPIT IS NOT A PERFORMANCE STAGE

"Preach the word; be prepared in season and out of season; correct, rebuke and encourage—with great patience and careful instruction." —2 Timothy 4:2 (NIV)

Devotional Thought:

#DearYoungPreacher, ministry is not a show. The pulpit isn't a stage for your ego or performance—it's a platform for God's truth. Don't chase applause. Chase assignment. You are called to preach, not perform.

People don't need another entertainer—they need a word that will shift their soul. Let your preaching carry weight, not theatrics. Let your delivery be authentic, not rehearsed. The power is not in the performance but in the presence of God.

Encouragement:

You don't need to impress—just obey. The Spirit will do the rest.

Prayer:

Lord, strip away every desire to perform. Let my preaching carry Your power and presence. Help me stay faithful to truth and led by the Spirit. In Jesus' name, amen.

Meditation Prompt:

Do you ever feel pressure to impress when you preach? Why?

Respond:

Write down one way you can make your next sermon more Spirit-led and less performance-driven.

_____

_____

_____

_____

_____

_____

_____

_____

_____

_____

_____

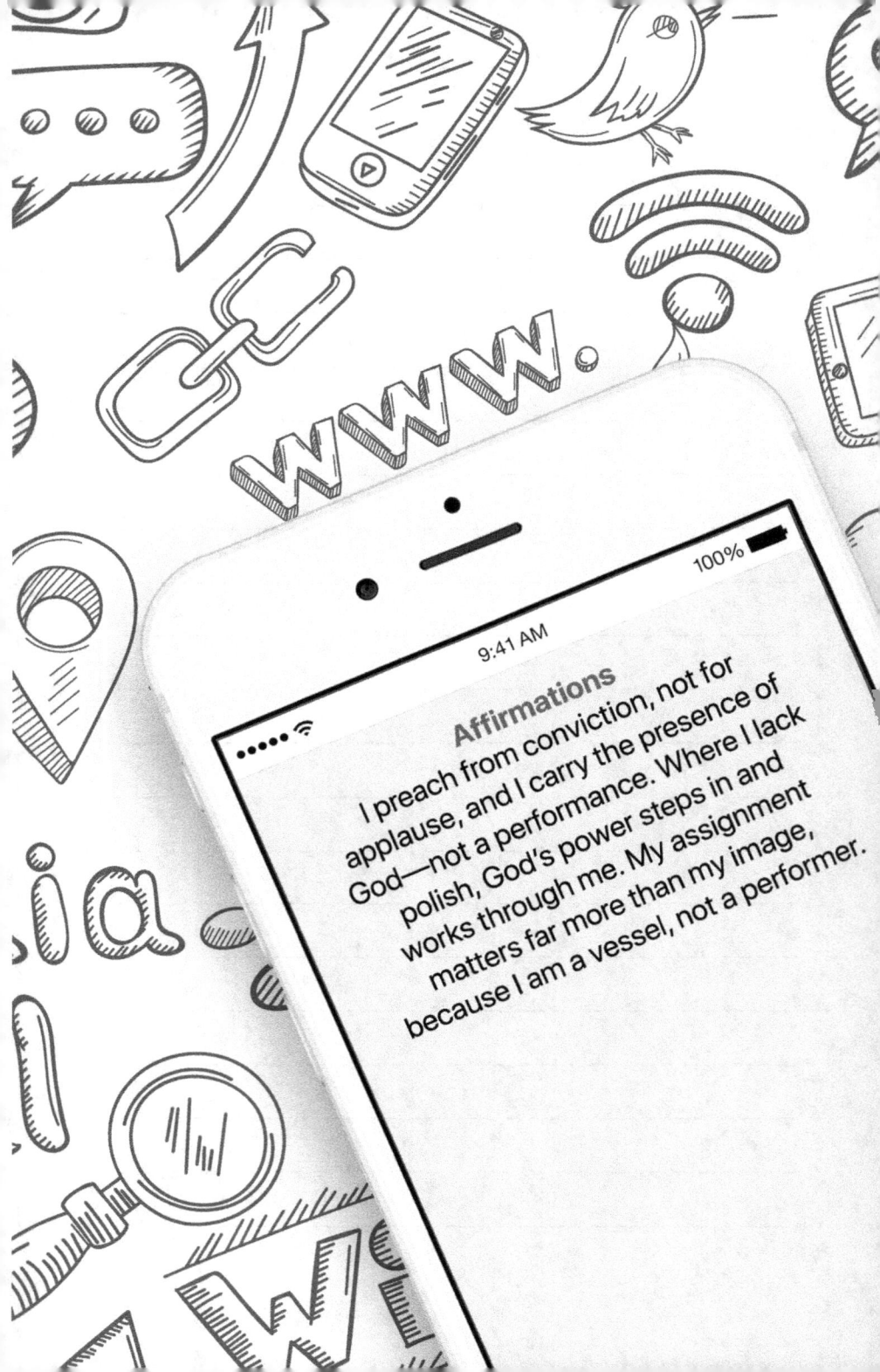

Affirmations

I preach from conviction, not for applause, and I carry the presence of God—not a performance. Where I lack polish, God's power steps in and works through me. My assignment matters far more than my image, because I am a vessel, not a performer.

DAY 18: YOUR VOICE MATTERS

"Do not let anyone look down on you because you are young, but set an example…" —1 Timothy 4:12 (NIV)

Devotional Thought:

#DearYoungPreacher, don't let age, insecurity, or inexperience silence your voice. God knew your age when He called you. You may not sound like everyone else, but you don't have to. Your voice is uniquely anointed to reach someone no one else can.

God isn't waiting for you to be older, louder, or more polished. He's waiting for you to be faithful. Lift your voice. Preach the Word. Let Heaven echo through your obedience.

Encouragement:

You don't need to sound like anyone else to be effective. Be authentically you.

Prayer:

Father, thank You for giving me a voice. Remove fear and insecurity. Help me to speak boldly and live faithfully. Use my voice to reach the ones You've assigned to me. In Jesus' name, amen.

Meditation Prompt:

What lie have you believed about your voice or calling?

Respond:

Write out a declaration of how you will boldly use your voice for God's glory.

_____

_____

_____

_____

_____

_____

_____

_____

_____

_____

_____

Affirmations

My voice is anointed and necessary. I am not too young—I am called by God for such a time as this. I speak with boldness, not fear, knowing that I don't need to fit in to be effective. God moves through my obedience, and His power flows through every word He gives me.

DAY 19: BE CAREFUL WHO LAYS HANDS ON YOU

"Do not be hasty in the laying on of hands, and do not share in the sins of others." —1 Timothy 5:22 (NIV)

Devotional Thought:

#DearYoungPreacher, impartation is real. Be careful who you allow to lay hands on you and speak into your destiny. Not every hand is clean, and not every voice carries truth. Protect your spirit.

This journey is sacred. Walk with discernment. Just because someone is famous or influential doesn't mean they're assigned to you. Wait on God's timing and guidance.

Encouragement:

You don't need every connection—just the right covering.

Prayer:

Lord, give me discernment to know who's assigned to speak

into my life. Protect my spirit from ungodly impartation and align me with leaders who carry Your heart. In Jesus' name, amen.

Meditation Prompt:

Have you sought validation from people God never assigned to you?

Respond:

Take time to pray over your spiritual mentors and relationships. Ask God for clarity and protection.

_____

_____

_____

_____

_____

_____

_____

_____

_____

_____

DAY 20: BE AN ANSWERED PRAYER, NOT JUST A GIFTED SPEAKER

"Then I heard the voice of the Lord saying, 'Whom shall I send? And who will go for us?' And I said, 'Here am I. Send me!'" —Isaiah 6:8 (NIV)

Devotional Thought:

#DearYoungPreacher, your calling is bigger than sermons—it's about service. People are praying for breakthrough, hope, healing, and clarity. You are not just a speaker—you are someone's answered prayer.

Before you step up to the mic, ask God who you're being sent to. See the crowd, but preach to the heart. Minister from compassion, not performance. This is soul work.

Encouragement:

Your calling is not just about how you speak, but how you love.

Prayer:

Lord, make me sensitive to the needs of those You've called me to. Let me be an answer, not just an echo. Fill my mouth with words that bring healing. In Jesus' name, amen.

Meditation Prompt:

How often do you consider the needs of others when preparing to preach?

Respond:

This week, ask someone what they need prayer for—and pray intentionally.

DAY 21: DON'T PREACH WHAT YOU DON'T PRACTICE

"You then, who teach others, do you not teach yourself?" — Romans 2:21 (NIV)

Devotional Thought:

#DearYoungPreacher, integrity matters. Preach from what you live, not just what you've learned. People can feel the difference between a practiced message and a lived testimony. Your life is your loudest sermon.

Let the Word cut you before it comes through you. Let it confront, comfort, and correct you. That's where the true power is. Be the message before you preach the message.

Encouragement:

You don't have to be perfect—but you do have to be real.

Prayer:

God, help me to live the Word before I preach it. Let my life match my message. Where I fall short, help me grow. Keep me honest and humble. In Jesus' name, amen.

Meditation Prompt:

Is there an area where your life and message don't align?

Respond:

Take inventory of your recent sermons. What's one area you need to strengthen to walk in alignment?

DAY 22: GRACE FOR THE GAPS

"Trust in the Lord with all your heart and lean not on your own understanding." —Proverbs 3:5 (NIV)

Devotional Thought:

#DearYoungPreacher, there will be moments in ministry when you won't have the right words, the quick solution, or the "deep" answer. That's okay. You were never called to be all-knowing—you were called to be faithful. You are not the Savior; you're simply the servant.

There is **grace for the gaps**—the spaces between what you know and what they need, between what's asked of you and what you feel capable of giving. It's in those very gaps that God shows Himself strong.

It's okay to say, "I don't know, but I'll stand with you in prayer." It's okay to pause, to listen, to ask for wisdom. People don't need you to be impressive—they need you to be **authentic**.

You don't have to be deep, you have to be **present**. You don't have to know it all, you just have to **point to the One who does**.

Encouragement:

Let go of the pressure to perform. God is not measuring your worth by your answers, but by your obedience and humility. Trust Him to fill in where you fall short.

Prayer:

Lord, thank You for being all-sufficient. Remind me that I don't have to carry the weight of knowing everything. Help me to trust You more deeply and rest in Your wisdom. Let my humility speak louder than my opinions. In Jesus' name, amen.

Meditation Prompt:

Where do I feel the pressure to "know it all"? How can I give myself permission to rest in God's wisdom?

Respond:

Write about a time when you didn't have the answer but had to show up anyway. How did God meet you in that moment? Reflect on what it taught you about trust, humility, and presence in ministry. Then, write a short prayer or declaration you can return to when you feel pressure to "have it all together."

_____

_____

_____

_____

Affirmations

I don't have all the answers—and that's okay. I am led by the Spirit, not by pressure or expectation. God alone is my source of wisdom and strength, and in humility, I make room for His clarity to guide me. I minister not from performance, but from total dependence on Him.

DAY 23: GUARD YOUR PRIVATE LIFE

"Above all else, guard your heart, for everything you do flows from it." —Proverbs 4:23 (NIV)

Devotional Thought:

#DearYoungPreacher, what happens behind the scenes matters. Who you are when no one is watching shapes your power when everyone is. Don't lose your soul protecting your platform. Guard your heart. Set boundaries. Keep your worship sacred.

You don't need to post everything. You don't need to share every thought. What's private is powerful. Stay rooted in the quiet place. Your fruit depends on it.

Encouragement:

Protect your peace. Protect your purity. Protect your relationship with God.

Prayer:

God, help me to value what is sacred and guard my heart from distraction and compromise. Keep me anchored in You when no one sees. Let my private life honor You fully. In Jesus' name, amen.

Meditation Prompt:

What private habits or boundaries need strengthening right now?

Respond:

Decide on one digital or relational boundary you'll put in place this week to protect your spirit.

Affirmations

I guard my heart and protect my peace, choosing to value the private place with God over public applause. I am disciplined in my unseen life, knowing that true fruit is rooted in the secret place. Even when no one is watching, I live with integrity, anchored in quiet faithfulness and devotion.

DAY 25: THE ANOINTING COMES WITH A COST

"But we have this treasure in jars of clay to show that this all-surpassing power is from God and not from us." —2 Corinthians 4:7 (NIV)

Devotional Thought:

#DearYoungPreacher, everyone wants the anointing, but not everyone wants the crushing. Oil flows from pressure. The anointing you carry is tied to the pain you've survived, the prayers you've prayed, and the surrender you've walked through.

Don't despise the process. God's preparing something in you that others will feel when you speak. And it won't be your talent they feel—it will be His touch.

Encouragement:

The cost is high, but the oil is worth it.

Prayer:

Lord, thank You for trusting me with the crushing. Help me to carry the anointing with humility. Let it never be about my gifting, but always about Your glory. In Jesus' name, amen.

Meditation Prompt:

What painful experiences have shaped your calling?

Respond:

Write about a moment of breaking that God used to make you more usable.

_____

_____

_____

_____

_____

_____

_____

_____

_____

_____

Affirmations

My crushing produces oil, and God is shaping me through every trial I face. I carry the anointing with humility, knowing that my pain is not wasted—it has a divine purpose. Through it all, I am being refined for greater impact, prepared for what God has called me to carry.

DAY 26: MINISTRY IS A MARATHON, NOT A SPRINT

"Let us not become weary in doing good, for at the proper time we will reap a harvest if we do not give up." —Galatians 6:9 (NIV)

Devotional Thought:

#DearYoungPreacher, don't burn out trying to prove yourself. Ministry isn't about quick impact—it's about faithful endurance. Slow down. Pace yourself. Rest is not rebellion—it's reverence for your body and calling.

The fruit you're looking for takes time. Stop comparing your pace to others. Trust God's timing. Stay steady, not flashy.

Encouragement: Longevity is built through wisdom, not weariness.

Prayer:

God, teach me to run with endurance. Help me to trust Your pace and rest in Your provision. Give me strength for the journey and grace for the slow seasons. In Jesus' name, amen.

Meditation Prompt:

Are you sprinting in ministry when God is calling you to pace yourself?

Respond:

Schedule intentional rest time this week. Protect your rhythm.

Affirmations

I am built for endurance, embracing God's perfect pace for my life. My rest is sacred and necessary, renewing me for the journey ahead. I don't compete with others—I simply continue faithfully. Even in the slow seasons, I remain steadfast and committed to the calling God has placed on me.

DAY 27: HONOR THE ASSIGNMENT EVEN WHEN IT'S HARD

"Whatever you do, work at it with all your heart, as working for the Lord, not for human masters." —Colossians 3:23 (NIV)

Devotional Thought:

#DearYoungPreacher, not every assignment will feel exciting. Some will feel obscure. Some will stretch you. But every assignment from God is holy. Preach to five like you would five hundred.

Don't chase platforms—chase purpose. Stay faithful to the place God planted you. Promotion comes through obedience, not ambition.

Encouragement:

Honor is the posture that unlocks more.

Prayer:

Lord, help me honor the season I'm in and the people You've called me to. Keep me from frustration and comparison. Let me serve faithfully wherever You place me. In Jesus' name, amen.

Meditation Prompt:

Are you waiting for a "bigger" opportunity instead of honoring your current one?

Respond:

Write down three blessings about your current assignment—even if it's hard.

_____

_____

_____

_____

_____

_____

_____

_____

_____

_____

DAY 28: PROTECT YOUR FRIENDSHIPS IN MINISTRY

"A friend loves at all times, and a brother is born for a time of adversity." —Proverbs 17:17 (NIV)

Devotional Thought:

#DearYoungPreacher, don't lose yourself in ministry and forget the friends who strengthen you. Ministry can be lonely if you isolate. You need people who love you when you're not preaching, posting, or performing.

Choose friends who protect your humanity, not just your image. Laugh. Rest. Be vulnerable. You need real ones to survive this calling.

Encouragement:

Friendship is a form of warfare—don't do life alone.

Prayer:

God, thank You for true friends. Help me to be honest, connected, and covered. Let me nurture the relationships that refresh me. In Jesus' name, amen.

Meditation Prompt:

Are you making room for friendships that nurture your soul?

Respond:

Reach out to one friend today just to check in—no ministry talk.

_____

_____

_____

_____

_____

_____

_____

_____

_____

_____

_____

_____

Affirmations

I am not meant to walk this journey alone; I intentionally cultivate friendships that fuel my soul. I make space for joy and vulnerability, knowing that my circle strengthens my spirit. God surrounds me with the right people to support, encourage, and uplift me along the way.

DAY 29: DON'T GET CAUGHT UP IN COMPARISON

"Each one should test their own actions. Then they can take pride in themselves alone, without comparing themselves to someone else." —Galatians 6:4 (NIV)

Devotional Thought:

#DearYoungPreacher, comparison is a thief. It will rob your joy, cloud your focus, and blur your assignment. Someone else's success is not your failure. Their lane is not your lane.

Celebrate others without competing. Focus on what God has placed in your hands. Stay committed to your own growth.

Encouragement:

Clarity comes when comparison dies.

Prayer:

Lord, free me from the trap of comparison. Remind me that I am uniquely called and completely equipped. Let me celebrate others and stay faithful to my assignment. In Jesus' name, amen.

Meditation Prompt:

What triggers comparison in your heart?

Respond:

Write down what makes your calling unique and worthy of focus.

DAY 30: PREACH WITH ETERNITY IN MIND

"Set your minds on things above, not on earthly things." — Colossians 3:2 (NIV)

Devotional Thought:

#DearYoungPreacher, every sermon is a seed with eternal impact. Don't preach for popularity. Preach for legacy. Let your words echo in Heaven. Speak to souls, not just situations.

What you say today can shape someone's eternity. Keep the eternal goal in mind. Heaven rejoices when you stay focused.

Encouragement:

Eternity is the goal—everything else is temporary.

Prayer:

God, keep my eyes on what matters most. Let every word I speak carry eternal weight. Help me to lead souls closer to You with every opportunity I have. In Jesus' name, amen.

Meditation Prompt:

Are your sermons rooted in eternity—or popularity?

Respond:

Revisit a recent message. How did it impact eternal thinking?

DAY 31: YOU WERE BORN FOR THIS

"Before I formed you in the womb I knew you, before you were born I set you apart; I appointed you as a prophet to the nations." —Jeremiah 1:5 (NIV)

Devotional Thought:

#DearYoungPreacher, you didn't stumble into this. You were chosen for this. Every moment, every mistake, every lesson prepared you for this divine assignment. God saw this day before you were born.

Walk in it. Own it. You are not an accident—you are anointed. This calling was written in your DNA. Go forth boldly.

Encouragement:

You are not just called. You are chosen.

Prayer:

Father, thank You for Your perfect plan. I embrace my calling with confidence and humility. Use me in ways that glorify You. I was born for this. In Jesus' name, amen.

Meditation Prompt:

What has kept you from fully embracing your calling?

Respond:

Write a declaration of acceptance and surrender to your calling.

_____

_____

_____

_____

_____

_____

_____

_____

_____

_____

_____

_____

www.ingramcontent.com/pod-product-compliance
Lightning Source LLC
Chambersburg PA
CBHW050329010526
44119CB00050B/726